GILA MONSTERS

BY MELISSA ROSS

Apex is distributed by North Star Editions:
sales@northstareditions.com | 888-417-0195

Produced for Apex by Red Line Editorial.

Photographs ©: Shutterstock Images, cover, 1, 4–5, 6–7, 10–11, 12, 13, 14, 15, 16–17, 18–19, 20, 21, 22–23, 25, 29; iStockphoto, 8–9, 26–27; A. Cosmos Blank/Science Source, 24

Library of Congress Control Number: 2022920185

ISBN
978-1-63738-545-6 (hardcover)
978-1-63738-599-9 (paperback)
978-1-63738-704-7 (ebook pdf)
978-1-63738-653-8 (hosted ebook)

Printed in the United States of America
Mankato, MN
082023

NOTE TO PARENTS AND EDUCATORS

Apex books are designed to build literacy skills in striving readers. Exciting, high-interest content attracts and holds readers' attention. The text is carefully leveled to allow students to achieve success quickly. Additional features, such as bolded glossary words for difficult terms, help build comprehension.

TABLE OF CONTENTS

CHAPTER 1

MONSTER MOUTH

A Gila monster crawls across the ground. Its long tongue flicks in and out. Suddenly, the lizard smells an animal.

Gila monsters can't move very fast. They sneak up on their food to catch it.

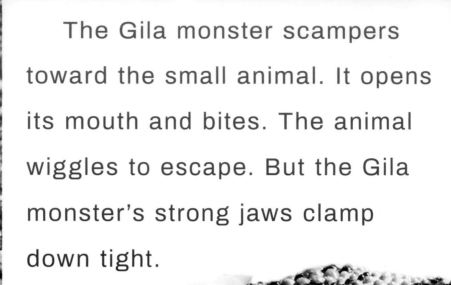

The Gila monster scampers toward the small animal. It opens its mouth and bites. The animal wiggles to escape. But the Gila monster's strong jaws clamp down tight.

When a Gila monster bites an animal, it might hold on for more than 10 minutes.

FAST FACT

A Gila monster's bite has **venom**. The bite is also strong enough to crush small animals.

The lizard swallows the animal whole. Then it scurries away. It finds a shady spot to rest.

Gila monsters do not spend much time out in the open.

WADDLE WALK

Gila monsters have short legs. So, their walk is like a waddle. When they move, their tails swing side to side. That helps the lizards balance.

CHAPTER 2

A HOT HOME

Gila monsters are large lizards. They can grow 22 inches (56 cm) long. Like all lizards, Gila monsters are **reptiles**.

Adult Gila monsters usually weigh 3 to 5 pounds (1.4 to 2.3 kg).

Gila monsters usually live in areas with some small plants.

Gila monsters are desert animals. They live in Mexico and the southwestern United States. Their **habitats** are grassy and rocky.

FAST FACT

Gila monsters are named after the Gila River. They are commonly found there.

The Gila River runs through New Mexico and Arizona.

Gila monsters are covered in scales. The scales look like beads. Their patterns provide **camouflage**. The lizards can blend in with rocks and sand.

Gila monsters are usually black with orange, pink, or yellow spots and stripes.

Sometimes Gila monsters hide under rocks.

STAYING HIDDEN

Gila monsters spend a lot of time in homes called burrows. If it is too hot, they might only come out at night. In winter, they spend almost all of their time in the burrows.

CHAPTER 3

DESERT DINING

Gila monsters are **carnivores**. They hunt birds, mice, and small lizards. Sometimes they also eat eggs.

Gila monsters can eat animals that are up to one-third of their body size.

Gila monsters leave their burrows to hunt. They do not see well. So, they use their tongues to find **prey**. Their tongues pick up scents in the air.

A Gila monster's tongue is forked at the end.

FAST FACT

Sometimes Gila monsters crack open eggshells. They drink the liquid inside.

Gila monsters mainly eat in spring and summer. They might not eat during colder months.

When Gila monsters find prey, they bite. Venom comes out through their teeth. Gila monsters keep biting while the venom kills their prey.

A BIG MEAL

Gila monsters can eat a lot in one meal. Then they might wait months before eating again. Gila monsters only need a few big meals each year.

Gila monsters store energy in fat in their tails. They use this fat for energy when they are not eating.

CHAPTER 4

LIFE CYCLE

Gila monsters **mate** in spring or summer. Two males sometimes fight for a female. They wrestle for hours. The strongest one wins.

When they are not mating, Gila monsters usually live alone.

Gila monsters dig holes in the sand to lay their eggs.

A female Gila monster lays
up to 12 eggs at a time. She
buries the eggs in sand. Then
she crawls away. The eggs hatch
several months later.

FACING DANGER

Gila monsters have **predators** in the wild. Coyotes, hawks, and owls might eat Gila monsters. The lizards are also threatened by humans destroying their habitats.

Coyotes are members of the dog family. They are mostly found in North and Central America.

Gila monster **hatchlings** look like small adults. They have venom like adults, too. They can live on their own right away.

Hatchlings are usually a few inches long. After three to five years, most are fully grown.

FAST FACT

Gila monsters can live up to 20 years in the wild.

COMPREHENSION QUESTIONS

Write your answers on a separate piece of paper.

1. Write a few sentences describing how a Gila monster catches and eats prey.

2. Do you think a Gila monster would make a good pet? Why or why not?

3. What part of a Gila monster's body releases venom?

> **A.** its teeth
>
> **B.** its scales
>
> **C.** its tongue

4. What could happen if humans continue destroying Gila monsters' habitats?

> **A.** More Gila monsters could have babies.
>
> **B.** Gila monsters could start to eat predators.
>
> **C.** Gila monsters could begin to die out.

5. What does **clamp** mean in this book?

The animal wiggles to escape. But the Gila monster's strong jaws clamp down tight.

    A. let go
    B. hold firmly
    C. make noise

6. What does **threatened** mean in this book?

Coyotes, hawks, and owls might eat Gila monsters. The lizards are also threatened by humans destroying their habitats.

    A. left alone
    B. given help
    C. put in danger

Answer key on page 32.

GLOSSARY

camouflage
Colors or markings that help animals blend in with the area around them.

carnivores
Animals that eat meat.

habitats
The places where animals normally live.

hatchlings
Young animals that have recently hatched from eggs.

mate
To form a pair and come together to have babies.

predators
Animals that hunt and eat other animals.

prey
Animals that are hunted and eaten by other animals.

reptiles
Cold-blooded animals that have scales.

venom
A poison made by an animal and used to bite or sting prey.

BOOKS

Ringstad, Arnold. *Totally Amazing Facts About Reptiles*.
   North Mankato, MN: Capstone Press, 2018.

Sabelko, Rebecca. *Gila Monsters*. Minneapolis: Bellwether
   Media, 2019.

Tobler, Elise. *Gila Monsters Have a Deadly Bite!* New York:
   Enslow Publishing, 2021.

ONLINE RESOURCES

Visit **www.apexeditions.com** to find links and resources
related to this title.

ABOUT THE AUTHOR

Melissa Ross is the author of *Forensics for Kids* and other
educational books for children. She is fascinated by the
interesting animals we share our planet with, and she enjoys
sharing the wonder of them with young readers.

INDEX

ANSWER KEY:
1. Answers will vary; 2. Answers will vary; 3. A; 4. C; 5. B; 6. C